Data Science

What You Need to Know About Data Analytics, Data Mining, Regression Analysis, Artificial Intelligence, Big Data for Business, Data Visualization, Database Querying, and Machine Learning

Contents

INTRODUCTION 1

CHAPTER 1: WHAT IS DATA SCIENCE? 3

CHAPTER 2: WHAT EXACTLY DOES A DATA SCIENTIST DO?...........14

CHAPTER 3: A LOOK AT WHAT DATA ANALYTICS IS ALL ABOUT .22

CHAPTER 4: WHAT IS DATA MINING AND HOW DOES IT FIT IN WITH DATA SCIENCE? 31

CHAPTER 5: REGRESSION ANALYSIS 40

CHAPTER 6: WHY IS DATA VISUALIZATION SO IMPORTANT WHEN IT COMES TO UNDERSTANDING YOUR DATA? 47

CHAPTER 7: HOW TO WORK WITH DATABASE QUERYING 55

CHAPTER 8: A LOOK AT ARTIFICIAL INTELLIGENCE 60

CHAPTER 9: WHAT IS MACHINE LEARNING AND HOW IS IT DIFFERENT FROM ARTIFICIAL INTELLIGENCE? 65

CHAPTER 10: WHAT IS THE FUTURE OF ARTIFICIAL INTELLIGENCE AND MACHINE LEARNING? 75

CONCLUSION 81

Introduction

The following chapters will discuss everything that you need to know when it comes to working in the field of data science. This world has changed, and with the modern technology that we have, it is easier than ever for companies to amass a large amount of data on the industry, on their competition, on their products, and their customers. Gathering the data is the easy part, though. Being able to sort through this data and understand what it is saying is going to be a unique challenge all on its own. This is where the process and field of data science can come in.

In this guidebook, we are going first to take a look at what data science is all about. We can explore some of the basics of data science, along with a few of the benefits that you are likely to see when you work with this process. With that in mind, we can also spend some time looking at the exact things that a data scientist as a professional would do while on the job daily.

From there, we are going to dive right into some of the things that you can do with data science, and the different aspects that come with it to ensure the professional can get through all of the information, and fully understand it in no time at all. Some of the topics that we are going to explore that fit in with this idea include what data analytics is about. For instance, the importance of data mining, what a regression analysis is all about, as well as the different types of that mining and analysis. We'll look at why data visualization can be important when we want to understand the enormous amount of information found inside our data.

Once we have had some time to explore the different aspects that come together in the world of data science, we will delve deeper, exploring a few more topics before ending this guidebook. We will look at information about artificial intelligence and machine learning. We will learn how these are helping to take some of that data from before, using it to create smart, intelligent computers and other systems that we can use in our daily lives.

In this part, there is a lot to discuss about these two options. There is so much potential for growth in these areas, especially as the world begins to accept this science more, and when users start seeing the benefits of putting them to use. We will – in particular - look at what artificial intelligence is all about, what machine learning is, and how it can be different from artificial intelligence. Finally, we will look at where these two topics are likely to go in the future.

There is so much that we can explore and learn about when it comes to the world of data science, and this guidebook is here to help you navigate through these specialties. You will see just how important the ideas of data mining, data analytics, and even artificial intelligence are to our world as a whole today. When you are ready to learn more about data science and what it is all about, make sure to read through this guidebook to help you get started.

Chapter 1: What is Data Science?

The first thing that we need to focus on is what data science is all about. Data science is going to be a very detailed study of the flow of information from a large amount of data that is presented to a company. In our modern world, there is information everywhere that we turn. Companies can set up their machines, their social media accounts and other social media products to collect an enormous amount of data from their customers. This data is much broader in scope than we will see with anything that has been done in the past.

While gathering all of this information may seem like a goldmine, the problem comes when we try to figure out what we are going to do with all of that data. It does not do us much good to hold onto that information, without any idea of what to do with it, or what is found inside. Because we have so much information present in this set, it is hard for a single person to go through and find the trends and the patterns that are in there by themselves.

Data science is here to handle this kind of problem. It is going to step in to help us figure out what is found in the information, and even how to store the information. With the help of artificial intelligence and machine learning, which we will talk about a bit later, we will find that data science will be able to go through the information and find what trends are there, especially the ones that are hidden.

When it comes to data science, we are going to be able to obtain some meaningful insights from raw and unstructured data, which is then going to be processed through skills that are business, programming, and analytical. Let's take a look at more about what this data science is all about, why it is important, and some of the different parts of the data science cycle.

The Importance of This Data Science

To start with, we need to figure out why this data science industry is so important. In a world that is turning more to the digital space than it ever did before, organizations are going to deal with a ton of data, data that is unstructured and structured, on a daily basis. Some of the evolving technologies that we can look at have enabled us to save a lot of money, and smart storage spaces have come up in order to store a lot of this data until companies can get to it.

Currently, there is a huge need for skilled and certified data scientists to help go through this information and see what is found inside. In fact, when it comes to the IT industry, these data scientists are going to be among the highest-paid professionals out there. According to Forbes, the annual salary for the average data scientist is almost $110,000.

Why is this industry paying so much? Because it is in high demand and many companies are looking to find qualified professionals who can gather, store, and look through all of the data that they have available and provide them with predictions, information, and help in using this information to make good business decisions. The number of professionals who are actually able to process and derive valuable insights out of the data is few and far between, so they are in high demand.

Furthermore, there are a lot of requirements out there in order to become a data scientist. Because of all this, there is going to be a 50 percent gap in the industry when it comes to the demand for data scientists versus the supply of these professionals. This is why it is so important to learn more about data science and how this kind of topic is changing up so many industries throughout our world.

With that in mind, we need to focus a bit more on data science and all of the different parts that are going to come with it. In the last few years, we have been able to see a large amount of growth in one field that is known as the Internet of Things (IoT). Because of this growth, we see that 90 percent of the data in our current world has been generated by and for this IoT field.

Each day, we see 25 quintillion bytes of data generated for companies to use, and this number will grow at an even faster rate as IoT continues to thrive. This extraordinary amount of growth in data can be useful for a lot of companies to learn about their customers, focusing on the best products to release next, and working toward the customer service they would like to provide. All of this data is going to come from a variety of sources that will include:

Sensors are set up in shopping malls in order to gather up the information of the individual shopper.

Posts on the various platforms of social media can send back information to the company.

Videos that are found on our phones and digital pictures are taking in more data than ever before.

Companies are able even to get some good information when they look at some of the purchase transactions that come when people shop online and through e-commerce.

All of this data, no matter its source, is known as big data. As you can imagine, with all of the various sources for information, companies are going to be flooded with more data than they know what to do with. It is impossible for an individual to go through and do all of the work on their own. This is why it is so important to really know what we should do with all of this data and the best way to utilize it in order to make good business decisions in the future.

It is here that the idea of data science is going to start showing up into the picture. Data science is going to bring together a ton of skills that we can find in the world of business, including business domain knowledge, mathematics, and statistics. All of these are important because they are going to help an organization out in a variety of ways, including:

Helping the company learn new ways where they can reduce costs each day.

It can help the company figure out the best method to take to get into a new market that will be profitable for them.

This can help the company learn about a variety of demographics and how to tap into these

It can help the company to take a look at the marketing campaign that they sent out there and then figure out if the marketing campaign was actually effective.

It can make it easier for the company to launch a new service or product successfully.

These are just a few aspects of business that this big data is going to be able to help us out with. This means that no matter what kind of industry will be able to use the ideas of data science in order to help them learn about their customers, their marketing campaigns, their products and more and lead up to more success for the company.

How Some Top Industry Leaders Use Data Science

In this section we are going to take a look at some data science can actually be used, and how some of the industry leaders, such as Amazon and Google, are already using data science in order to help them get ahead of the competition in many different areas. IT organizations have a big need in order to address some of their expanding and complex data environments to help them identify some new sources of value, exploit the opportunities that are there, or find ways to optimize and grow themselves in an efficient manner.

Here, one of the biggest deciding factors for the organization is what value they are going to be able to extract from their data repository using analytics, and how well they can present this information. Let's look at some examples of the big leaders of the industry and how they are using data science, and data scientists, to help get things done.

First on the list is Google. Google is going to be the biggest company that is hiring data scientists right now. This is because a lot of the products that Google is releasing right now, and a lot of the features that they are offering to their customers are drive-by data science, especially artificial intelligence, and machine learning.

Amazon is another good example of how we can work with this. Amazon is seen as a global e-commerce and cloud computing giant that is also working on lots of projects in the data science world and hiring data scientists all the time. They need these professionals to help them learn more about their customers and the needs of these customers while enhancing the geographical reach of both their cloud domains and e-commerce domains as well, along with some of the other goals they have to drive business.

And we can also look at Visa and see how they are working with data science as well. Visa is known as an online financial gateway for a lot of companies, and in one day, they can do transactions that are worth hundreds of millions. Due to this fact, the need for qualified and professional data scientists is high at this company so that they can keep customers and companies safe, and generate even more revenue in the process, check out transactions that could be fraudulent, and customize some of the services and products based on the requirements of the customer.

The Life Cycle of Data Science

The next thing that we are going to take a look at here that can be kind of fun is the idea of the data science life cycle. For a better understanding of how this whole process of data science is going to work, we need to actually look at what is known as the life cycle of this data science, and how it is going to influence a lot of different things for the business.

To start, let's say that we have a Mr. X and he owns a retail store. His whole goal here is to help improve the sales that his store sees by identifying the main drivers of those sales. To help Mr. X accomplish this new goal, he has a few questions that he needs to answer, and these are going to include:

Which products in the store are going to bring him the most profit on a regular basis?

How are some of the promotions that he is doing in-store working at making sales?

Are the different placements of products that are used in-store deployed in an effective manner?

The primary aim that we are going for here is to answer these questions, which is really going to have a lot of influence on the project and the outcome that it has. Because of this, Mr. X decides to hire on a data scientist to sort through all of the data that is available and determine the right course of action along the way. Let's use the life cycle of data science, which we are going to discuss below, to help us to solve this problem and see how the owner can do to improve sales and revenues.

Data Discovery

The first part of this data life cycle is known as data discovery. This part is going to include all of the ways that someone is able to discover data from a variety of sources. The data can come in many different forms, including in a format that is unstructured, such as in images or videos. But it can also come in a more structured format that would include files of text. There is also the possibility that it can come from a relational database system as well.

Right now, organizations are also able to take this a step further and are using social media to their advantage. It is not uncommon for a business to look at data they can obtain from social media, and other similar sources to help them to understand some of the mindset of their customers better than ever before. It is during this stage that the object is to take a look at some of the data that has been collected, and then figure out the best course of action to boost sales. Some of the things that we may see in this stage that are affecting sales for this business will include:

Store location

The locations and the promotions that competitors on the market are offering.

Product pricing

Product placement

Promotions

The hours that the business is open.

The staff and their knowledge about the products.

Keeping these factors in mind, we can develop a bit more clarity on the data, and it takes some time to help us actually find the data that we need. When we are all done with this stage, we can collect the data, from all of the different sources, especially any that are going to work with the elements that we have listed above, and then can move on to the second stage.

Data Preparation

Once we are done going through and discovering the data and finding it from all of the different sources that we can collect it from the second stage is going to include preparing the data. There is quite a bit that will go on in this stage, including converting the disparate data into a format that is common (if you have some text and some images, you need them to all be the same time to finish this process), so they all work together.

This part of the process is going to involve collecting data that is clean and then inserting the defaults where necessary, the ones that are suitable. In some cases, based on the kind of data you are working with, it could involve methods that are more complex, such as identifying some of the missing values through the process of modeling.

Once the cleaning of the data is done, the next step is to start integrating that data and then seeing if you can create your own conclusion from the set of data for analysis. This is going to involve the integration of data, which means that we need to merge two, and sometimes more, tables of the same objects, but storing different information, or it could mean summarizing fields in a table using aggregation. Basically, our goal here is to have a chance to explore, and even understand what values and patterns are hidden in all of this data so we can use it later.

Mathematical Models

We also need to learn about some of the mathematical models that are found in our projects of data science, and how these models are there to drive our products. These models are going to be planned out ahead of time and built by data professionals so that they can suit the needs that are specific to the business. This could include a lot of different things depending on what the business needs the most, but some of the areas that could be included are logistics, linear regressions, statistics, differential and integral calculus and more.

There are a variety of tools and options that you can use when it comes to working on these mathematical models but setting them up in the proper manner is going to ensure that we actually can work on the data and learn what is inside. In some cases, you can also do fine with just one model, but depending on the complexity of the model and what your end goal is all about, it is possible that you will need to work with more than one model.

If more than one model is needed, the data scientist is going to spend some time creating a unique group of models. After they have been able to measure out the models, the professional can then make any necessary revisions to the parameters and then fine-tune them for the next run with modeling. This could include a few different steps in order to get the work done, based on how long it takes until the professionals know they are working with the very best model for the job.

During this step, the data scientist is going to build up the mathematical models that they need, based on what the business really wants. This could be something like figuring out which product between two or three is the most profitable, whether the store is seeing success with their product placement, and so on. The success of the model, and whether or not it is working, often depends on what we are trying to monitor in the process.

Getting Things Going

Once we have taken the time to prepare the data the right way, and we have built up the models that we need to use, it is time for us to move on and get the models working. These models do us no good in theory; we have actually to put them to work to get the right results. There might be a lot of discrepancies along the way, and sometimes troubleshooting is going to be needed, and this is why a data scientist will need to tweak their models a few times before they get the most accurate results. In this stage, we are going to work to gather information and then derive the right outcomes based on the business requirements that are necessary at that time

Communication

This is going to be our final step, but don't think that this makes the step any less important or that you can skip over it any time that you would like. In this step, you need to be able to communicate the findings that came out of the data and out of your model. The data scientist will be the liaison between various teams, and if they are successful, they need to be able to seamlessly communicate the findings they got in the other steps to the key stakeholders and decision-makers in the organization. This helps to get actions taken based on that data, as well as based on the recommendations that the data scientist is going to give out at this time.

If we are still working with Mr. X from the retail store before, you could take the information that you found through the other steps, and then communicate and recommend certain changes to the business strategy that will help Mr. X to make necessary changes. If the work was done in the proper manner, your recommendations would read the data in the proper manner, and Mr. X - after implementing those recommendations - will be able to earn the maximum amount of profit.

The Components of Data Science

In this part of our discussion, we need to get a look at some of the different components that come with data science. There are actually quite a few that need to come together and work in order to get the most out of data science fully. The first component that comes with data science is going to be the various types of data. The raw set of data is going to be the foundation of our data science journey, and it can be found in various different types. The two main types will include structured data, which is often going to come in tabular form, and then the other one is going to be the unstructured data, which is going to include PDF files, emails, videos, and images.

The second component that we are going to find when we look at data science is programming. You have to come up with some programming in order to make those mathematical models that we talked about earlier and to get them to really sort through the information and make predictions. All of the analysis and management of the data is going to be done by computer programming. The two most popular languages that are used in data science will include R and Python, so learning one of these can be helpful.

Next on the list: probability and statistics. Data is going to be manipulated in a manner that it is able to extract information and trends out of that data. Probability and statistics are going to be the mathematical foundation that brings it all together. Without having a good idea and a lot of knowledge about these two topics, it is possible that you will misinterpret the data, and will come up with conclusions that are not correct. This is a big reason why probability and statistics are going to be so important to the world of data science.

We also have to take a look at the idea of machine learning when we are looking at data science. When someone is working through all of that big data and everything that is contained inside of it, they are also going to use a lot of the algorithms that come with machine learning. This can include the methods of classification and regression at the same time.

Someone who wants to work as a data scientist has to have a deep understanding of machine learning and a lot of the different algorithms that come with this kind of learning. Otherwise, they are going to misinterpret the data they have and can run into some problems. Machine learning is so important to this kind of field because it helps to take all of that available data, and the set of data is often quite large and can help them to make predictions and learn valuable insights in the process.

And finally, another key component that comes with this data science is big data. In our modern world, raw data is something that we can compare to crude oil. When we look at the way we extract refined oil from the crude oil, by using data science, we can extract useful and helpful information from our raw data. Some of the different tools that are already available for this that can help us process some of the big data will include Apache Spark, R. Pig, Hadoop, and Java, to name a few.

Many companies have become efficient at gathering large amounts of data about their stores, about their products, and about their customers. But because they are so efficient at gathering this information up, they now have so much of it that the process of diving in and sorting through all of it seems intense, and no one person can do it on their own. Even if a team tried to go through that information, it would take too long, and important information and trends that are needed to make smart decisions would be left behind and missed in the process.

This is where the idea of data science can come in. With the help of the right algorithms and more, the data scientist is able to sort through all of the big data and can find some of the big trends that are hidden inside. Often this is done in a manner of minutes, and maybe hours if there is a ton of data, through machine learning algorithms in the process.

These algorithms are quick and efficient and can provide the business owner with the tools and information they need to make sound business decisions in no time. For many companies, this is the method they are going to use in order to learn more about their customers, increase their sales, and gain an edge over the competition.

Chapter 2: What Exactly Does a Data Scientist Do?

The world - when it comes to data science and big data - can sometimes seem really complex when we are on the outside looking in. IN business, there are a lot of people who already know what the big data analysis is all about, and that it involves someone going in and collecting the ever-growing about of data that is being generated all of the time, and then using this information to come up with insights that are meaningful and will help the business to grow. But what this is going to involve in terms of the day to day job of the data scientist is a completely different thing to consider.

 We are going to spend some time in this chapter looking at some of the things that the data scientist is going to do on a day to day basis, and what their job really entails. This can help us to understand why they are in such high demand overall, and why their job is so important to so many different companies right now.

Some of the Key Capabilities of a Data Scientist

The term data scientist is able to cover up many roles through a variety of organizations and industries, whether we are looking at the government, at finance, or even in academia. While there are a lot of capabilities that need to come into play, there are going to be three main ones that everyone who works as a data scientist has to be able to understand before they get started.

First, the data scientist has to understand that all of the data has some meaning. Often, we are going to overlook the fact that we have all of this data, and it actually means something, and it is important for us to understand what that meaning is all about. We have to be able to look beyond the numbers that are there, and then get a better understanding of what these numbers stand for. Without this understanding, then we are not going to be able to gain the insights that we need. Understanding the data that is presented to us is more of an art, and it is so important. All of the rest will not make sense or help you that much if you aren't able to understand the meaning of the data.

The next thing that a data scientist has to keep in mind is that they need to understand the problem that has to be solved, and how the data relates to and will be able to help out with that. Here we are going to spend some time opening up the tool kit to find the right analytics and approaches and algorithms that you can use in order to work with that data. There are literally hundreds of different techniques that you can use in order to get the data to solve your problems.

There are a lot of options to choose from out of your tool kit, and you have to pick out the right one. You can work with decision theory, control theory, game theory, and operations research, for example, and all of these have been around for a long time. Once we have had a chance to understand the data, and we understand what kind of problem we want to solve with that data, then it is possible to pick out the right tool, or the right algorithm, and get the solutions we want.

And finally, a data scientist has to have some kind of understanding of engineering. This is not really about understanding and then delivering the infrastructure that was required to perform these analyses. It isn't going to do us much good to solve the problem if we haven't first gone through and created the infrastructure to deliver the solutions in an effective manner, in an accurate manner, and at the right place and time.

Being a data scientist who can do their job correctly is going to be more about paying attention to all three of these capabilities. You have to pay attention to the kind of data you have and where it is coming from, along with what it all means. You need to understand the problems that should be solved, and know-how the different algorithms with machine learning can fit in with this. You have to have good knowledge when it comes to engineering so that you can come up with the right solutions to the problem.

We also have to remember with this one that all of this does not mean we have to kick out the idea of specialization. It is important to note that it is virtually impossible for someone to be an expert in all three of these areas, plus all of the little sub-areas that come with each of them. You should have some general knowledge when you work in this field but being an expert in all of them is going to be pretty much impossible.

This opens up the door for someone to specialize in one of the areas. As long as you also hold onto an appreciation for all three of them, you are going to be just fine and can do well in this field. For example, even though you could primarily be the engineer or the person who works with the algorithms, if you do not have a good understanding of all the parts, and you can't figure out the problem you want to solve, or what the data is, then you will make decisions that are bad and not smart for the business.

Some of the Key Qualities That Show Up in a Data Scientist

In terms of some of the personal qualities that come with this kind of professional, we need to start out with a sense of curiosity. You have to be curious about what the data is going to tell you, and how you can use that information to solve problems. Communication skills are going to be another critical component, as well. Data scientists have to spend a lot of their time talking to other people, such as the customers so that they can figure out what the problem is that they should solve, or even talking to vendors of data to find out what they can provide. This puts the data scientist into the position of being the middleman, and this means that communication is going to be so important.

There are a ton of different personality types that decide it is a good idea to go into data science, so each one you are going to meet will do things in their own way. This is part of what makes this field so exciting and will ensure that those who get into this field can remain an asset to the company, while still enjoying a lot of the work that they are doing in the process.

With this in mind, we need to take a look at some of the simple terms; a data scientist is going to help a company analyze the data for actionable insights. Some of the specific tasks that can be done with the help of a data scientist will include:

They are responsible for identifying some of the data analytics problems that are going to be used in the proper manner, offer some of the greatest opportunities to the organization.

They are going to be responsible for determining the correct sets of data and the variables that need to be used.

They are responsible for helping a business collect a ton of data, both the unstructured and the structured kind, from a large variety of sources to use in decision making.

They are responsible for cleaning and validating the data that they can find in order to make sure that the data is accurate that the data is complete (at least as much as possible), and that there is uniformity in the data as well.

They are responsible for devising and then applying various algorithms and models to mine the stores of big data that they helped to collect in the first place.

They are going to be responsible for analyzing the data to identify patterns and trends.

They will be able to interpret the data in order to discover the solutions and the opportunities that are there and will help the company to succeed the most.

They are responsible for being able to communicate any of the findings that they got with that big data. This information is going to be shown to the stakeholders with the help of visualization tools and any other means necessary.

To help us see the general view of this data scientist, we can look at them as a professional who knows how to extract the meaning from and also interprets the data that they have. This is going to require them to use both tools and methods that come to them from machine learning and statistics, along with some common sense. This person is going to spend a lot of their day collecting, cleaning, and then munging the data they have. This process is going to take in a lot of persistence overall, along with skills in statistics and engineering to get it all done. The data scientist must also contain the skills for understanding some of the biases in the data, and for debugging logging output from the code.

Once the data scientist has been able to get that data into shape, they will then do an analysis of the data that is more exploratory. This is going to be done with the help of data sense and visualization. The professional is going to find any patterns that are there, build up models, and work with the algorithms. This is sometimes done with the intention of understanding the usage of a product and the overall health of how the product is doing. Sometimes the information will serve as a prototype that will be put in with the product at some point.

In some cases, this professional is going to design their own experiments, and they will be critical when it comes to some of the decision making that is driven by data. They can also communicate with a lot of other people in the company, including the leadership, engineers, and other team members using data visualizations and clear language to make sure that everyone is on the same page and understands what is going on in that data.

What do I need in order to start with this career choice?

If you have been reading through this guidebook so far, it is likely that you are curious about what all it takes to become a data scientist and add this as your own career choice. Some of the things to look at to help determine if this is the right kind of career path for you will include:

Do you have, or are you willing to work towards, a degree in something like marketing, management information systems, computer science, statistics, and mathematics?

Do you have a lot of work experience in these kinds of areas?

Do you already find the idea of collecting and analyzing data interests you?

Do you like to do work that is more individualized and enjoy spending time problem-solving?

Are you able to do well with communicating with a lot of different people, both in a visual manner and verbally?

Would you like to find some methods that help broaden out your skills and do you enjoy taking on new challenges?

If you were able to answer yes to most of these questions, then you may find that the field of data science is going to be the right one for you. It takes a sharp and critical mind, as well as someone who is really curious and likes to find the answers that they need within the information.

Data scientists must have a good amount of knowledge in statistics and math, in addition to the information that we talked about above. A lot of the work that you do with your algorithms and other parts of data science is going to include these two things.

Another thing that you need is a natural curiosity, along with critical and creative thinking to go along with it. You have to be willing to look at the data and think about all of the things that you can do with the data. What undiscovered opportunities lie hidden within? Most of these professionals are good at connecting the dots, and they have a big desire to search out the answers to questions that have not yet been asked so that they can find the full potential that comes with the data.

An advanced degree for this kind of work is also pretty common. These professionals are going to have higher degrees than a lot of the fields out there, with about 88 percent of them having a master's degree as a minimum, and 46 percent have a Ph.D. This helps to ensure that they have the right knowledge and experience necessary in order to handle some of the complexities that come with their job.

During your education, it is often best to have a background that includes some computer programming. Since you need to use programming to help make up the algorithms and models for mining all of that big data, many languages can work for this. Understanding the basics of Python will make a big difference since this is the one that is most commonly used.

Some data scientists are also like entrepreneurs. Business strategy is important, whether you are an individual doing the work or you work on a team with other data scientists along the way. It is hard for you to be successful in this kind of career, or for any other professional to take off in it, if you are not able to first devise some of your own methods and build up your own infrastructures to slice and dice the data in a way that can help you find out new things, and figure out the new visions or the future out of all the data you have collected.

And the final part of the puzzle that is nice for a data scientist to have is good communication skills. These professionals have to spend a lot of time talking about the complex ideas they have and sharing these with people who need to know the information, but who are not well-versed in data science. This means that in this capacity, you need to take some of the complex topics that you are working on and explain them in a way that others will be able to understand as well.

There are several methods that you can utilize that will make this easier, such as data visualization tools. But your verbal communication skills need to be strong as well so that you can clearly tell the right story and make it easy for others to understand what you are doing with your work, and how this kind of data science is going to be beneficial to your needs.

The work of a data scientist can be complex. While it may seem like they just have to sort through some data and then are done for the week, there are a lot of different parts that have to come into the mix in order for these professionals to do their job properly. They need to know how to gather the data. They need to know how to clean the data and write out algorithms and models that will help them go through the data and find good trends and patterns that can make predictions. They need to be able to communicate in a clear and concise manner so that others can understand what these findings mean to them.

Chapter 3: A Look at What Data Analytics Is All About

While we are on the topic of data science, it is also important to take a look at data analytics. This is going to be a subset of our data science that we talked about earlier, and it is going to be important when it comes to handling the data that we can gather, from various sources, and then figuring out what it all means. You can hold onto all of the data that you want, but if you don't understand what that data is trying to tell you, then the data is pretty much worthless to you and your company. This is where the process of data analytics is going to come into play.

To start, data analytics is going to be the science of taking raw data and analyzing it in order to make some conclusions about that information. Many of the processes and the techniques that reused with this have been automated into algorithms and mechanical processes that will work over the raw data and turn it into something that humans can read through and understand.

When the techniques are used in the proper way, data analytics will help us to see trends and metrics that would be lost in other situations, lost in all of the data that you are holding onto. This information is then going to be used to help optimize processes to help increase how efficient a system or a business can be overall.

Now that we know a bit about the broad meaning of data analytics, it is time to get into some of the different parts of it, and how we can use it to our advantage. The term data analytics is going to be broad, and it includes many diverse types of data analysis. Any type of information that can be subjected to techniques of data analytics to get inside that can then be used by humans to improve something about their business will fall under this umbrella.

Let's look at an example of this. Many manufacturing companies are going to spend time recording the work queue, downtime and run time for the different machines that they are working with. They will then take the data that contains this information and use it to better plan how and when the workloads should happen. This helps the machines get as close to their peak capacity as possible, saving time and money in the process.

This is just one of the tasks that data analytics is going to be able to help out with, even though preventing bottlenecks in production is a good thing to pay attention to. Gaming companies are going to be able to use this process in order to set up the right reward schedules for players which is done in a way that ensures the majority of players stay active in the game rather than dropping off and rarely using it. Another example is a content company. They can use the various parts of data analytics in order to keep their customers clicking, watching or even reorganizing the content so that they can get the clicks and the views that they need.

We have to remember that data analysis is a complex process, and not one that you can just glance at and come up with the answers. If you do this, then it is likely that you are missing out on a lot of important information within that large set of data. Some of the steps that you can use in order to conduct a proper data analysis will include:

We start out this process by determining the requirements of the data, or how the data has been grouped together. There are a lot of possibilities here including the data being separated out by things like gender, income, demographics, and age. The values of the data could also be numerical, or they may be divided up by category as well.

Then in the second step of this is the process of collecting our data. There are a ton of different sources where you can get all of this information. It could be from your employees, from sources in the environment, online sources like surveys and social media, and even from your computer system.

Once the data has been collected, and you are sure you have the data that you need, it is time to organize the data Since you are collecting it from a variety of sources, you have to make sure that it is organized in a manner that makes sense, and one that the algorithm will be able to read through quickly and find the trends to make predictions from when you get to that step.

You can choose what method you would like to use when you organize the information. You can work with a spreadsheet or try some kind of software that is good at handling data that is statistical.

Once you have been able to organize the data the way that you would like, it is time to clean it all up before the analysis happens. This means that the data scientist has to go through and scrub the data and check that there are no errors or duplications that are found in the information, or that the data is not incomplete. This step takes some time, but it ensures that everything is fixed and ready to go before you even start.

The key points to remember from this part is that the data analytics is going to be the science of taking your raw data and then analyzing it to help make conclusions based on that information. The processes and techniques that are used with this have already been automated in many cases, and you will see this in use with algorithms that can take the raw data and make it work for human consumption. The main reason that a business would want to use this kind of process, and to analyze the data they have, is because these analytics are going to help the business to optimize their customer service to others and optimize their performance.

Why Does this Analysis Matter?

With this in mind, you probably already understand a little bit about why the process of data analytics is so important, and why a business would want to get this done with all of the information that they have gathered. They can use the information that is in the data, but often there is just so much data, and it comes from so many different locations, that it needs a bit of work in order to really see what is there, and to use it to make accurate predictions along the way based on the data.

The process of data analytics is going to be important because it is going to really help any kind of business that uses it to optimize their performances implementing it into the business model means that a company will be able to reduce their costs, simply by having the process identify more efficient ways for them to do business, and because it can help them to store in an efficient manner large amounts of data.

In addition to all of this, a company is going to be able to use the process of data analytics to make decisions that are so much better for their company. This analysis is also one of the best ways to analyze customer trends, and customer satisfaction, which is going to make it easier for the business to offer new and much better, products and services than they would without this kind of analysis happening.

The Different Types of Data Analysis

While we may look at this and assume all of the analysis is going to be the same, and that there isn't any variation that will show up, this is just not true. There are a few types of analysis that you can work with based on what you want to see happen in the end, and what your goal is when you work through the data. The four basic types of data analytics that most data scientists are going to work with include:

Descriptive analytics. This is one that will take the time to describe what has happened in the data over a chosen period of time. You may look at things like whether the number of views has gone up, or if the sales for your company are higher or lower than they were in the previous month for a product.

Diagnostic analytics This is the one that will focus more on why something has happened, or the root of how your business is doing. This one is helpful, but it will involve data inputs that are more diverse and a bit of hypothesizing in the process. For example, did you have a slow sales week because the weather was bad, and no one went out shopping? Or did something go wrong with one of your marketing campaigns and that is why sales are struggling?

Predictive analytics. This one is going to be used to help predict what is most likely to happen in the near future, based on the information that we have at our disposal right now. What happened to the sales last year when the summer was warm? How many weather models are going to tell us that there will be a hot summer this year, and we should prepare for more of what we saw in the past.

Prescriptive analytics. This one is going to be responsible for suggesting a course of action that the company should take. For example, if the likelihood of a hot summer is measured as an average of five weather models and this likelihood is above 58 percent, then it is likely that you should add in more shifts to handle the sales if this is something that has happened in the past.

When we use data analytics, it is going to underpin many of the quality control systems that are found in the financial world, and other companies as well. An example includes the program of Six Sigma that has taken over helping to reduce waste and increase creativity and efficiency. If you are not able to measure something properly, whether it's your own weight or the number of defects that you are getting per million during the line of production, then it is hard to optimize the work that you are doing.

Every business wants to optimize things, and they want to make sure that they are getting the most out of all the work they do along the way. Data analytics is one of the best ways to make this happen. It helps the company to really see what they can do, and ensures that they actually have some data, some hard facts behind all of their decisions before they even start.

Data analytics, as we discussed a bit before, is going to be a field that spends its time analyzing sets of data that the company has been able to gather from a variety of sources. When this analysis is done, we can then draw some conclusions from the information that was provided. It is a very popular strategy that is growing, and more industries over time are starting to jump on board and use it, from the healthcare field to the financial field and every industry in between.

Data scientists are going to spend a lot of time challenging themselves to not just draw a conclusion from the numbers they see but they also need to find the most efficient and useful way to analyze and use the information. This has to be done quickly. If it takes the data scientist five years to go through the data, then their work is not worth it. Trends change quickly, and there will be many more sets of data that come in during that time. The analysis must be done quickly, hopefully at a rate that is able to keep up with all of the data that keeps coming in during this time.

As the ways that we can gather up and store our information changes, companies need employees who not only can take a look at the data, but who can also keep themselves up to date on the most current methods of handling these numbers so the company can get the most use out of that information. The data scientist will also need to be able to keep a good eye on this information for future needs.

This is a lot of work and is not always as easy as it seems. The demand to handle all of this data and perform accurate and timely analysis on that information is going higher and higher, and the supply of professionals who can do this kind of work is not able to keep up. This is true in almost any field that is looking for a data scientist right now. Organizations are leveraging and analyzing an extraordinary amount of data, much more than they were ever able to do before. They want to continue doing this because it helps them to make decisions that are smart and driven by data, but it is something that takes a professional to do, and this can be a challenge to find the employees who will be able to handle the work for them.

The Benefits of Doing an Analysis of the Data

When it comes to performing a data analysis, there are a ton of benefits that any company, no matter what industry they are in, can receive from this process. It may seem like a long and drawn-out process that is hard to work with, and many companies fall into the habit of just collecting the data and then have no idea what they should do with it. But actually, analyzing the data that you have, and seeing what is inside can benefit your company in many different ways. Some of the best benefits that your company can receive from completing a data analysis will include:

Helps you to understand your customers better. All businesses want to understand their customers. This is the best way to make more sales and increase revenue. But how are you supposed to know what the customer wants, and what is going to convince them to come to your store compared to going over to a competitor? This data analysis can take information from customer surveys and customer habits and help you make more informed decisions to provide better customer service to increase sales as well.

Helps you to know what trends are going on that you should follow for your business. There are always trends that go on in any market, but these trends are often shifting and changing at really fast rates that are hard to keep up with. Using a data analysis can help you to catch on to some of the trends ahead of time, making it easier for you to really meet the needs of your customers.

It helps you to know your product better. Sometimes, this data analysis can be used to help you know which products are doing the best and why. You may find out that one product is actually doing better than you thought, or that you should start selling more of a similar product to increase sales.

It can help make smarter business decisions overall. It is always best if you can have data and information behind all of the decisions that you make for your company. The data analysis helps you to comb through all of that information and see what is there before you make any decisions about your company.

It is great for beating out the competition. Companies who are willing to take a look through all of that data, and see what trends are hidden inside are the ones to catch on to new information faster and can beat out others in the industry.

These benefits can help us to really see how important this data analysis can be for the whole company, and why it is in such high demand in almost every industry that is out there. For some smaller companies who are not choosing to gather as much data, and can work on a more local level, it may be too time and cost consuming. But for larger companies that need to work against a lot of competition, and who are juggling a lot of different parts, this can be the best option to help you get started with helping your business grow in more ways than one.

~~Who~~ is using data analytics?

Another topic that we can explore is the idea of who is using data analytics already. The number of companies who can use this kind of process, and who are seeing a lot of benefits with this kind of process may surprise you. To start, you will find that the hospitality and travel industries are going to use this data analytics. Turnarounds for this industry are quick, and with data analysis, they can collect a lot of data from their customers and learn where the problems are. When the problems are found, it is easier for them to make changes that result in better service for everyone.

Healthcare is another industry that is using these ideas. Healthcare is able to combine the use of high volumes of data, whether this is structured or unstructured data, and then will use the process of data analytics to help the companies make decisions quickly. This could make a huge difference for many of the patients who utilize this system on a regular basis.

Even retailers can use data analysis. Think about all of the information that a retailer is able to collect from their customers over time, and when they use the information properly, they can meet the always-changing demands of their shoppers. The information that is collected by these retailers and then analyzed is going to help them to see what trends there are, can make better recommendations, and all comes together to increase the profits that are seen by the company.

Data analytics is going to be important no matter what kind of industry you are in at the time though. The examples above are just a start to the list, and any company or industry that collects data from social media, their customers, or from other sources, will need to do some kind of analysis on that data to see what is inside. It is so beneficial to many companies to do this, and skipping out on it, or thinking that it is not that important can really cause harm to your company.

Inside this information, you can learn what your customers want, what the complaints are and how you can fix them, what products to release to your customers, how to beat out the competition, what others are doing and so much more. Deciding not to look through this information, and ignoring all that it has to say is going to be a big mistake, and could leave you behind as your competition takes the lead simply because they knew it was important to do a data analysis ahead of time.

Chapter 4: What is Data Mining and How Does It Fit in with Data Science?

Another topic that is important for us to spend some time discussing when it comes to data science is the idea of data mining. Data mining is going to be a process that is used by many companies in order to take some of the raw data that they have, and then turn it into information that is actually useful for them to use. By using the software, and a few other tools along the way, that can help them to look for patterns in all of the data they have collected, a business is able to learn a lot more about their customers.

So, why would a business want to learn all of this extra information about their customers? When the business does data mining properly, they will be able to develop marketing strategies that are more effective, can help to decrease their own costs, and even increase sales at the same time. Data mining is going to depend on the effective collection of data, along with computer processing and warehousing to get it all done.

One thing to note here is that the processes of data mining are going to be used to help us build up machine learning models. These models that rely on machine learning can power up applications, including the recommendation programs found on many websites, and the technology that is able to keep search engines running.

Some of the History That Comes with Data Mining

The process of going through all of the data that we have and trying to find some of the hidden connections that are there so that we can predict some of the future trends is actually something that has been around for a long time. While this is sometimes known as "knowledge discovery in databases," the term of data mining is not going to be something we heard about until the 1990s. But the foundations that come with it are going to have three different disciplines of science that are going to be intertwined with one another. These three points are going to include:

Statistics: This is going to be the numeric study of the relationship that is found in the data you are using.

Artificial intelligence: This is going to be the human-like intelligence that a machine or a type of software is able to exhibit when the right kind of coding is done.

Machine learning: These are the different algorithms that you can use on the data in order to have that data reveal its trends and help you make some predictions.

What was once an older topic is now newer again, as the technology that comes with data mining is evolving, even more, to help keep pace with all of the potential of big data, and thanks to the idea that computing power is becoming more affordable.

Over the past ten years or so, some of the advances that have happened in the speed and power of processing have made it easier to move beyond the time-consuming, tedious, and manual practices. We can instead work with a type of data analysis that is automated, easy, and quick. The more complex sets of data that we can collect, the more potential there is for data mining to find some really great insights that can help with the growth of your company.

You will find that there are a lot of companies that are going to work with data mining to discover the right relationships between demographics, promotions, and price optimization to the risk the competition, the economy, and more that can affect their customers.

Some of the companies that are using this kind of technology are going to include insurers, telecommunications providers, manufacturers, banks, and retailers. When these companies use data mining in the proper manner, it is going to be able to affect each aspect of their business, including customer relationships, operations, revenues, and business models.

How Data Mining Works

So, why is data mining such an important process to focus on? You will see the staggering numbers when it comes to the volume of data that is produced is doubling every two years. Just by looking at unstructured data on its own, but just because we have more of this information does not mean that we have more knowledge all of the time. With the help of data mining, you can do some of the following tasks:

Sift through all of the noise, whether it is repetitive or chaotic, that is found in your data.

You can understand better what is relevant in all of that information, and then make good use of the information to help you assess what outcomes are the most likely for your needs.

It can help you to accelerate the pace of making decisions that are informed and driven by data, and more likely to help your business to thrive and grow.

 Now we need to take a look at how this data mining works. We are not able to just grab the data and have these trends shown to us without any additional work. This is where data mining is going to come into play. Data mining is going to involve us exploring and then analyzing a large block of information in the hopes of getting trends and patterns out of that information that is meaningful. We can use the process of data mining in a variety of ways based on what industry the company is in, what they do to serve the customer, and so much more.

For example, data mining can be used to help us discern the opinion, and the sentiment of our users can help with detecting fraud, credit risk management, email filtering with spam, and database marketing to name a few things. All of these are important to many industries and can help them to become more efficient in their jobs while being able to serve the customer even better in the long run.

The process of data mining is going to be broken down into five different steps. In the first step, the company is going to collect the data, and then make sure that it is loaded up properly into their data warehouse. When that is done, they will store and manage the data, either using the cloud or some of the servers they have in-house.

At this point, the IT professionals, management teams, and business analysts are going to access the data and then will determine the best way to organize that information. Then application software is able to come in and sort out the data, based on the results of the user. In the last step, the end-user is going to present the data and all of the findings that were done in the other steps, in a format that is easy to share and usually understand in the form of some kind of visualization like a table or graph.

The next thing that we need to work on is data warehousing and mining software. The programs that you use with data mining will work to analyze the patterns and the relationships that are found in the data, and it is going to do this based on the request of the user. For example, a company may use some of this software in order to create some new classes of information.

To help us illustrate this a bit more, let's imagine that we are a restaurant that would like to use the process of mining data in order to determine the best times to offer specials. The restaurant is going to look at all of the information it has been able to collect based on their specials and how these specials do at different times of the day, and then will create some classes based on when customers visit, and what the customers are going to order when they come to eat.

We can take this a bit further as well. In some cases, a data miner is going to be able to find clusters of information based on a logical relationship, or they may see if there are sequential patterns and associations to draw conclusions about trends in the behavior of the consumer.

Warehousing is going to be another important aspect of data mining. Warehousing is a simple process, and it is basically when a company will centralize their data into one program or one database, rather than having the information spread out between more than one place. With the warehouse for data, an organization may spin off segments of the data for specific users to look over and analyze on a regular basis, and for the specific users to use when they would like.

However, we can also see that the analyst can do another thing during this process as well. For example, sometimes an analyst may start with the data that they would like, and then they can go through and create a data warehouse that is based on those specs. No matter how a business, or even some other entities, organize their data, they use it to support the processes for making decisions with the management of the company.

With this in mind, we also need to take some time to explore examples of data mining along the way. A good example of this is grocery stores. Many of the supermarkets that we visit on a regular basis are going to give off free loyalty cards to customers. These are beneficial to the customers because it provides them with access to prices that are reduced, and other special deals that non-members at that store are not going to be able to get.

But these cards are also going to be beneficial for the store as well; it is going to make it easier for the company to track which customers are buying what, when they are in the store making the purchase, and at what price they are making the purchases for. After receiving all of this data and having a chance to analyze it the stores can then use this kind of data to offer customers coupons targeted to those buying habits, and they decide when to put certain items on sale, or when it is best for the company to sell them at full price.

This is a great way for both parties to win. The customer is going to enjoy that they can potentially save money and so they will sign up for it. The store is going to enjoy that they get a chance to learn more about the customers and set prices at a point that will bring in more people and make them the most money possible.

There are a few concerns that can sometimes come up when we look at data mining and what it is all about. Some people are concerned about data mining because they worry about the company using the information in the wrong manner. It could also be an issue if the company is not getting a good overall sampling of their information, and then make decisions that are wrong the wrong information in the process.

There are a few key takeaways that we can work here to help us get more out of data mining. Data mining is going to be the process of analyzing a large amount of information in order to help us discern the patterns and the trends that are inside. There is likely a lot of information that is going to be present for a business, and they can get that information from a large number of sources. But just having this information is not going to be enough to help the business get the results that they want.

Instead of just collecting the information and letting it sit there, the company actually needs to be able to find what is inside of all that information. There is likely a lot of topics to discuss inside that information, and you can use it to find trends, and make predictions that are driven by data. This makes the decisions better for your company and makes it more likely that you are going to be able actually to see success with it.

Another thing to consider is that data mining is going to be used by corporations for a lot of different things. The way that the company decides to use the information is going to depend on what they need to accomplish, what they gathered the information for, and more. The company can choose to use this information to help them learn more about what the customer is the most interested in and what they want to buy get. It can even come in handy when we talk about spam filtering and fraud detection.

Who uses data mining?

Data mining is going to be at the heart of many efforts for analytics through a variety of disciplines and industries. In fact, almost everyone is able to use this kind of process to help them sort through the abundance of information that they are storing and to ensure they get accurate predictions and patterns shown out of it.

The first industry that can benefit from data mining is going to be communications. This is definitely a market where the competition is tight, but the answers that are needed to stand out from the crowd are going to be found in your data about the consumer. Telecommunication and multimedia companies can use these analytic models to help them make sense of the mountains of data on the customer they have collected, which will help them to predict the behavior of the customer. This may also help in offering campaigns that are highly targeted and more relevant than ever before.

Insurance companies will often work with this data mining as well. With all of that analytic know-how, these insurance companies are going to be able to solve some complex problems when it comes to customer attrition, risk management, compliance, and fraud, to name a few. Companies have been able to use techniques from data mining to price products in the most effective manner across business lines and to find new ways to offer products that are competitive to customers who already use them.

Next on the list is going to be education. Education can benefit through the process of data mining, and data science as a whole, in many ways. With unified and data-driven views of student progress, it is easier for educators to predict the performance of their students, often before they even get to the classroom, and the teachers can use this information to develop strategies for intervention to keep them on course and doing well.

Data mining comes into play here because it helps the educators to access data on the student, predicts their level of achievement, and can help the educator figure out which students, or even which groups of students are going to need some extra care and attention in the process.

Manufacturing can also benefit when it comes to working with data mining. Aligning supply plans with demand forecasts is going to be essential, as is the early detection of problems, quality assurance, and investment in brand equity along the way. In many cases, with the help of data mining, these manufacturers can predict the wear of production assets and come up with a good schedule of maintenance ahead of time. This helps them to plan ahead and get the work done before a breakdown in the machine happens, maximizing uptime and keeping the production line going and on schedule as much as possible as things go through the day.

We may also see the use of data mining when it comes to banking and the financial world. There are already a number of automated algorithms out there that help banks better understand their base of customers, as well as the billions of transactions at the heart of this whole system. Data mining is able to help with these financial services and the companies that run them by providing a better view of the risks in the market, can help to find fraud faster, manages the obligations the institution has for regulatory compliance, and can ensure that the company gets optimal returns on all of their marketing investments to the customer.

And finally, we can take a look at how data mining is used in retail. Retail companies can take in a lot of information over all of the various customers they work with throughout the year. This results in a large database of the customers, which holds a lot of hidden customer insight that will help you to improve relationships with these customers, optimize the campaigns that you do for marketing, and can even help you to forecast the sales that you can expect in the future.

Through models of data that become more accurate all of the time, these retail companies can offer campaigns that are more targeted. This ensures that they will find that perfect offer that will actually reach the right customer, hopefully at the right time, and will end up making the biggest impact on that particular customer.

All of these industries may be seen as very different, but they do all come together and work to show us just how prominent data mining and data science really are, and why we would want to use these in our own work on a regular basis. It may seem like a lot of work and something that we don't want to waste our time on, and we may wonder if perhaps there are easier and better ways to handle all of the data we want to work with, but when it comes to gathering up some of the useful and relevant pieces of information inside a large set of data, data mining is one of the best choices to go with.

And the final point that we need to take a look at here is the idea that data mining programs are helpful because they are going to break down the patterns and the connections that are found in the data, and they can get this work done based on the information that the user is going to be able to provide or request at the time.

Chapter 5: Regression Analysis

As you work with a few of the different parts that come with data analysis, you are likely to run into the idea of a regression analysis. This is going to be one of the techniques that you can use with predictive modeling, and it is going to help us look at the relationship that is there between a dependent variable, which is the target, and an independent variable, which is the predictor. This is a big technique that is going to help us with time series modeling, especially with forecasting and the causal effect relationship that will show up with our variables. For example, we may be able to take a look at the relationship that shows up between rash driving and how many accidents happen on the road, and we can study this with regression.

This kind of analysis is going to be a very important tool that we can use for analyzing and modeling the data we want to work with. This analysis though, is meant to help us really see what kind of relationship is going on between at least two variables, but it is possible that more are going to be present. The best way to understand how this all will work together is through the following example.

Let's say that you are looking at a company and you would like to estimate the growth in sales they are having, based on the conditions that are going on right now in the economy. You have the data that is most recent for the company, and this information tells you that the growth in sales is actually about two and a half times the growth that we are currently seeing in the economy.

This is a great thing for the business because it shows how well things are going. We can use this kind of insight in order to make a prediction, assuming that all other things are going to stay constant, on how the future sales of the company will do, based on that past and current information.

There are a lot of benefits that come with using this kind of regression analysis. But the two most common benefits that we will see include:

This analysis is going to indicate to us those significant relationships that happen between both the independent variable and the dependent variable.

This kind of analysis is going to indicate the strength of impact on multiple independent variables on that one dependent variable that is in your problem.

Regression analysis is also going to allow us to compare the effects of variables measured on the different scales, such as the effect of price changes and the number of activities that you do that are promotional. These benefits will make it easier for the data scientist, or the data analyst, or the market researchers to eliminate and then evaluate the best set of variables that can be used for building up our predictive models.

With this in mind, we need to take a look at some of the different techniques that fit under this idea and how they are all used to help a company make some good predictions. These techniques are all going to be driven by three main metrics, including the number of variables you have that are dependent, the type of variable that is dependent, and the shape of the line for your regression. We will discuss these a bit more as we go through this chapter and see what is available at each part. To start, though, we need to take a look at the most common types of regression that you can work with, and how each of them will come into play with your work.

Linear Regression

This is actually one of the most common out of the modeling techniques. Linear regression is actually something that you will hear on a regular basis when it comes to doing some of the predictive modeling. With this technique, we will take the variable that is dependent and see that it is continuous. Then the independent variable, or more than one variable, can either be discrete, or it can also be continuous like the dependent variable. The nature of the regression line will be linear.

The linear regression that we are looking at is responsible for finding the relationship between our dependent variable, and at least one other independent variable, and it is going to use the best fit straight line to make it happen. A good way to visualize this is a graph with a lot of different dots, which will represent your data points. Then there is one line that goes through the middle, trying to match up with as many points as possible.

Of course, this line is not going to be able to hit all of the points of data. You are working with a straight line, and the points of data can be all over the place based on how they fit on the chart. But the idea here is to kind of find the average, and the point where many of the data points as possible are going to match up together and agree. Sometimes this line is slightly curved towards the end to catch a few more points, but it is best to see this one as a straight line, for now, one that is set up to take on as many points as possible.

A few points that we can keep in mind when it comes to the linear regression will include:

We need to see a linear relationship when it comes to our dependent and independent variables.

If you are working with multiple regression, it will suffer from autocorrelation and multicollinearity.

Linear regression is going to be a bad choice sometimes because it will be sensitive to the outliers. This can really affect the regression line, and in the end, if it is not handled in the proper manner, it is going to affect the forecasted values that you get.

This multicollinearity is going to increase how much variance is found in the estimate, and it will make it so that the estimate is sensitive to even small changes that happen in the model. The result of this is that the coefficient estimates that you try to work within this process are not going to be as stable as you may like.

When we are working with more than one independent variable, we can go with the stepwise approach, the backward elimination, and the forward selection to help you to deal with most of the important independent variables.

Logistic Regression

This kind of regression is going to be used to help us find the probability that an event is going to happen or fail. You will use this kind of regression when you have a binary dependent variable. This means that one of the answers is 0 and one is 1. You can choose which of these is true and which one is false, but those are the only two answers that are going to be able to show up in this case.

A few of the things that you can learn about the logistic regression to help make it a bit easier to use, and to see when it is best to work with this one compared to some of the others will include:

This kind of regression is going to be used for a lot of classification problems.

Logistic regression is not going to require us to have a relationship between the independent and dependent variables. It is able to handle the different types of relationships that show up because it is going to come in and apply the non-linear log transformation to the predicted odds ratio.

To make sure that the issues of underfitting or overfitting do not happen, we need to make sure that we include all of the significant variables. A good way to make sure that this happens is to use the stepwise method to estimate our logistic regression.

This kind of regression is going to require us to work with a sample size that is large. This is because the maximum likelihood estimates are not going to be as powerful or as accurate when we use some of the smaller sample sizes.

The independent variables should not be correlated with one another. We do have the option, however, to include interaction effects of categorical variables in our model and in our analysis if this is going to make a difference.

If the dependent variable ends up being multiclass, then it is going to be changed to a Multinomial Logistic regression instead of the logistic regression.

Polynomial Regression

Next on the list is going to be the polynomial regression. This is going to be when the power of the independent variable ends up being higher than 1. In this technique for regression, we will see that the best fit line is not going to be straight like what we talked about in the linear regression. Rather, this one is going to be more of a curve that tries to fit in more of the points of data to get a better result. To help us see more about how this type of regression is meant to work, let's look at a few key points:

While it is tempting to come in and fit a higher degree polynomial to get a lower rate of error, this is going to give us the result of overfitting in the process. Always plot the relationship to see the fit and then focus on making sure that the curve fits the nature of the problem.

It is a good idea to look out for the curve that happens towards the ends and then see whether these shapes and these trends make sense. Sometimes the higher polynomials are going to produce some weird results when you do the extrapolation.

Stepwise Regression

This is a type of regression that is going to be used at any time that we would like to deal with a lot of independent variables at the same time. In this kind of technique, the selection of these independent variables is going to be done using the automation process, which is going to involve us using no kind of human intervention in the process.

This feat may seem like a tall order, but it is achieved by the data scientist by observing some of the statistical values like AIC metrics, t-stats, and R-square to help us discern which variables are the most important. The stepwise regression is basically responsible for fitting the regression model by either dropping or adding in the co-variates one at a time, based on the criteria that you set up ahead of time. Some of the methods that fit under the term of stepwise regression that is the most commonly used will include:

Standard stepwise regression. This one is responsible for helping us do two things. It is going to help us to either remove or to add in predictors as is needed during all of the steps.

Forward selection. This one is going to take the predictor that is the most significant to start, and then will add in variables for each step as needed in the model.

Backward elimination. This one is going to start with all of the predictors already being found in the model and then will start taking some out. It will start out with the least significant variable during each step until you decide it is done.

The aim of working with this kind of technique for modeling is to maximize the prediction power with the minimum number of predictor variables. This one is a good one to choose when you want a method capable of handling higher dimensionality of the set of data.

Lasso Regression

This one is similar to some of the other regressions that you can work with, and it is also able to penalize the absolute size of the regression coefficients. In addition to doing this task, it is going to be able to reduce how much variability is found in your work and can improve the amount of accuracy that we can see with the models that rely on linear regression like what we talked about earlier.

The Lasso regression is going to be a bit different than the ridge regression, if you have worked with this one before, because it is going to use absolute values in the penalty function, rather than relying on the squares all of the time. This leads to penalizing or constraining the sum of the absolute values of the estimates, values that cause some of the parameter estimates to turn out as exactly zero.

The larger the penalty that we find, the further the estimates are going to be shrunk down before they get to absolute zero. This is going to result in variable selection out of given variables for this time. In addition to sharing this kind of information about the Lasso regression, we can also remember a few other key points about it, including the following:

The assumption of this kind of regression is going to be the same as least squared regression, but the normality is not something that we are going to assume.

This regression type is going to take your coefficients and then shrink them down to zero, which is going to make it easier when it is time to select some of the features.

This is a method of regularization, and you will see that it uses these kinds of formulas as well.

If you have a group of predictors that ends up being correlated really well, then the lass model is going to come into play and only pick out one of them to help make things happen. Any of the others that are there will be taken and shrink it down to zero.

As you can see here, there is a lot that you can consider when it comes to working with regressions and how they will be able to take the data that you have accumulated for a long period of time, and ensure that you can gain some powerful insights out of it. You have to choose which of the regression analysis you would like to work with, based on the type of data that you want to focus on, and what information you are trying to gather out of that set of data as well. Take a look at some of the regression formulas and information that we discussed above to help you really see what is available with this kind of analysis over your data.

Chapter 6: Why is Data Visualization So Important When It Comes to Understanding Your Data?

Now that we have a good idea of what data science is all about, and some of the different steps that need to be taken in order to find the data you want, search through it and come up with the insights that are found inside, it is time to understand the importance, and why we would want to use, data visualization in this process as well. Data visualization is going to be the presentation of data in a format that is either graphical or pictorial. Using this is going to enable those who make the decisions to see all of the analytics from the data presented in a visual manner.

While anyone could go through and read the information on the data and see what is inside on their own, often it is much easier to go through and actually see the information that is there is a visual form. With visualization that is interactive, it is easier to take the concept a bit further using technology to drill down into the graphs and charts to get more details in the process interactively changing up the data you see and the way it is processed to see what that means for the company.

Data visualization is going to be so important simply because of the way that the brain is able to process information. Using graphs and charts to help us visualize large amounts of data is easier compared to pouring over reports and spreadsheets all of the time. This process is a quick and easy way for us to convey concepts in a universal manner. You can often make small changes to the visuals to see what would happen in different situations as you move along. This makes it easier to compare several decisions to pick out the one that is best for your company.

In addition to making it easier for us to understand what is going on with the data, data visualization can help out with a few other tasks as well. Some of the tasks that data visualization is especially good at helping out with will include:

Identifying areas that need improvement or more attention.

Clarifying which factors are the most likely to influence the behaviors of the customer.

Helping you to understand which products should be placed in different locations throughout the store.

Making it easier to come up with predictions when it comes to sales volume.

There are already a lot of different ways that this data visualization is being used. Regardless of the size of the industry, or even what industry you are in, businesses can take data visualization and use it. Any time that you want to go through a large amount of data and figure out what is inside of it, using the other processes that we have already talked about in this guidebook, it is often a good idea to use data visualization along with it as well. This makes it much easier to understand what information is inside of the data and can help you to see better results in no time.

The first way that this data visualization is being used is to help us comprehend the right information quickly. By using a graphical representation of the information your business has, you can get a clear view of a large amount of data. The information is more cohesive, and it is written out or shown in a way that our brains can understand better than a long list or spreadsheet of numbers and data.

We can then look at these visuals and draw accurate conclusions based on what we see.

All data scientists and business owners will agree that it is much easier and much faster to analyze information that comes in some kind of visual format - such as a graph - than it is to look at this same information when it is in a spreadsheet or listed out for you to look over. Because of this fact, these visuals are going to make it easier for a business to address any problems that come up or answer the important questions in a timelier manner as well.

The next benefit that comes with using these visuals is that they are there to identify relationships and patterns, in an easy to read format, out of all the data you have collected. Even when we are using a very large and extensive set of data, we can start to make more sense out of it when it has been presented to us in a graphical manner. Businesses become better at recognizing what is there, seeing the relationships that show up, and even seeing which parameters are highly correlated.

Of course, sometimes the correlations are going to be easy to see, and we would be able to catch them in another format as well. But sometimes the correlations are harder to see, and we may miss out on them, and the important insights that we need, if we didn't first put the insights and data into a visual form. Identifying these kinds of relationships will make it easier for an organization to focus on areas that are the most likely to influence their other important goals as well.

The third benefit of using these visualizations and seeing how they are used is that, when a data scientist goes through the information properly and uses the right kind of visual, they are going to help us see the emerging trends early on. Using data visualization to help us discover trends, both in the market and in our own business, is going to really help to beat out the competition, especially if you are one of the first to see these trends before any of your competitors can jump on board.

When you can beat out the competition, simply by seeing the trends in the data you are already collecting, this is one of the best ways to improve your bottom line. With these visualizations, you will easily be able to see some of the outliers on the charts, especially the ones that will affect product quality or customer churn. From there, you can easily find ways to address these issues before they become really big problems that you have to handle and can ensure that you will be able to find new products and services that actually meet where your customers are.

And the fourth way that this is being used is to help communicate a story to others. Once a business has had a chance to take all of their data and uncovered some of the insights that are in there through visual analytics, the next step that we need to take a look at is the best way to communicate all of those trends and insights to other people. Using graphs, charts, and other visual representations that will make an impact and can showcase the data is going to be really important because it's more engaging, helps others to get the message easier, and can help make sure that everyone who sees the information is on board with the new plan.

With this in mind, we now need to go through and lay out the groundwork that is needed for data visualization. Before you try to implement any technology that is new, there are a few steps that we need to go through and take to make sure it all works out. For example, it is not enough to have a solid grasp of the data in front of you, and it is also important to have a good understanding of your goals, audience, and needs.

Taking the time to prepare your organization for this kind of technology to make these visualizations is not always as easy as you might like. Before you can implement it, there are a few things that you need to do first, including the following:

You need to have a good understanding of the data that you would like to visualize. This is going to include the size of the data you want to work with, and the cardinality or the uniqueness of the values of data in a column that you would like to use.

You need to be able to determine what you would like to visualize during this process, and what is the information type that you want to communicate in the charts and graphs and other visualizations that you would like to you.

You need to take some time to know your audience and then understand how these individuals are going to process their visual information. If you are showing this information to a group of data scientists, you may not need the visualization as much because they would know the tables of data and be fine. But if you are showing to the shareholders or to customers, or others who are not professionals in the data science world, then having more of these visualizations can be important.

You need to make sure that your vision is going to convey the information that you want to share in the best and the simplest form to your chosen audience.

Once you have been able to answer these initial questions about the data type that you have, and the audience whom you plan to show this information to, you then need to take some time to prepare for the amount of data that you would like to work with as well. Remember, many times a company is going to have their hands on a large amount of data, thanks to the ease of collecting this data in our modern world, and the inexpensive data storage that is available to them. This means that when you are working on creating your own data visualization, you are likely to have a ton of data that you need to sort through and use ahead of time.

Big data is great because it brings in more insights to the company and can help them to really see what their customers want at that time, but it does bring in some new challenges to the visualization that you are trying to do. This is because large volumes, different varieties, and varying velocities must be considered with this. Plus, it is common that the data is going to be generated at a pace that is much faster than what we can do while managing and analyzing it as well.

There are other factors that you need to consider as you go through this process, such as the cardinality of the columns that you want to add in and try to visualize. High cardinality is going to mean that in your data, there is already a large percentage of values that are unique. This could include something like bank account numbers because each of the account numbers is going to be a unique item. Low cardinality is going to be on the other side of things, and this means that there is going to be a large percentage of repeat values, such as in the column that would list out genders, either male or female, because those are the only two options.

While we are on this topic, we need to take a look at some of the most popular types of visualizations that you can use in data science. All of these can be great for helping you to sort through your data and see what it really means, in a visual form rather than with lots of words and numbers. The method that you choose to go with and the visualization that you decide to pull out is going to depend on your data and what you hope to learn from it. Some of the most common types of visualizations that you can use to understand better the data you have will include:

The scatterplot. This type of visualization is going to be used to help us find the relationship in bivariate data. It is often a good one to use to help us see correlations between two continuous variables.

Histogram: This one is going to show us the distribution that is there with a continuous variable. You can use this one to help you discover the frequency distribution that is there for one single variable when you are in an analysis that is univariate.

Bar chart: This can be called a bar plot or a bar chart. It is going to be used in order to represent data that is categorical with either horizontal or vertical bars. It is going to be a general plot that is going to help you aggregate the data that is categorically based on some function and the default that is going to be the mean.

Pie chart. You can use the pie chart to help represent the proportion of each category when it comes to data that is categorical. You are going to see this as a circle that is divided into slices based on the different parts so you can see how they will be in relation to one another.

Count plot: With the count plot, we are going to see something that is similar to what is possible with the bar plot, except that we only pass the X-axis and the Y-axis represents explicitly counting the number of occurrences. Each bar is going to represent the count for each category of species.

Boxplot: Next on the list is going to be the boxplot. This one is a good visualization to work with when it comes to seeing how the distribution of your variable is going to look. This is kind of a standardized way that we can display the distribution of data based on the five-number summary. This summary will show the maximum, the third quartile, the median, the first quartile, and the minimum.

These are the top types of visualizations that you can work with to help sort through and better understand the information that is hidden in your data. It is possible that you will be able to find other visualizations that work better for the data that you are trying to present, and it is just fine to work with these as well to help you see some better results. You have to choose the visualization option or method that works best for your needs.

Learning about these different options with visualization is so important it will help you to learn when is the best time to use each of these visualizations for data science, and will make it easier for you to really decide which one is the best based on what information you would like to show, and what data you are looking for.

Now all data is going to lend itself to the pie chart very well, for example. If you want to see how prices have gone up in the past ten years, then the pie chart would not be the best, but a line graph or a scatter plot may be the best option that you want to work with. But if you want to see how several parts can come together and how they will relate to one another, then you want to work with some of these visuals to help you understand what is going on, and to see the relationship right away, rather than having to try and read through all of the numbers to make it happen.

Visuals are going to be one of the best things that you can do when it comes to finishing up your work with data science. This is one of the best ways for you to take the information that you gathered, and the analysis that you did, and put it in a form that everyone, whether they are a data scientist or not, is going to be able to understand what you found out. When business leaders and owners want to see what work a data scientist did, and they are interested in seeing what options they should consider with their business and growth in the future, then these visualizations are going to be the best option to make this happen. Picking the right kind of visualization and knowing what it is going to be able to show out of your information, can make a big difference in how well you can show and explain your results.

Chapter 7: How to work with Database Querying

When you work with all of this data and the sets of data that are collected from a lot of different areas, it is likely that you will take that information and put it all in one database. This ensures that no matter what area you have used to collect the data, you will be able to put it all in one place and see it clearly and concisely. But once all of that large amount of data is in one place, you need an efficient method to help you to find the information that you need without wasting any time.

When you have potentially millions of data points or more, you do not want to go into the database and hope that you can find the one single item that you need. You don't want to try and compare and contrast all of those points either because there are just too many of them, or the database is going to be too large. With this in mind, one of the best things that you can do to make sure you find the information that you want, and something that can be done with your data analysis, is a database query.

This database query is going to help out because it can extract the data out of the database that you collected, no matter how big or small that database may be, and then it can format that data into a form that is readable for anyone. A query has to be written out in the language that is required by that database, and this usually means that we need to work with SQL or Structured Query Language. While Python is often used when it comes to some of the other parts that we need to do with data science, such as the algorithms that come with machine learning, we need to be able to learn how to work with SQL in order to work with any of the databases that we would like.

For example, when you would like to do the data out of a database, you need to start creating a query in order to request the specific information that is needed. Let's say that you have a table with your employees, and you want to be able to track the performance numbers of the sales and see how they are doing. You could do a query of the database for the employees who were able to record the highest amount of sales in a given period.

The first thing that we need to take a look at is the SELECT statement with SQL. This database query must follow the query format that comes with that database, and what the database is going to require. The most common format that is accepted by most databases will include the SQL format. This one is easy to work with, does not need a lot of coding experience, and has the power that is needed to get those queries done for you. SQL is a powerful language that even though it is simple and does not need a lot of parts, it has the capability of handling more advanced queries.

For example, using the SELECT statement is going to be enough to help you select the specific data that you need. For example, if you want to get the name and title from the database that you have, you can use the SELECT statement would come out as the following:

SELECT FirstName, LastName, Title FROM Employees;

A database has the potential to reveal complex trends and activities, but the power is only going to be harnessed through the use of the query. A database that is more complex will consist of more than one table that is storing all of the different points of data that you need. A query will allow you to filter the data into a single table, making it easier for you to analyze the information in a quick and efficient manner.

These queries are also going to help you to perform some calculations on the data, or you can automate some of the management tasks for that data. You can also review some of the updates that are present in the data before you try to commit them into the database, ensuring that the data is exactly how you would like it to be in the end.

To keep this process simple though, we need to remember that in the terms used with a database, the query is going to be the thing used in order to get data for you out of the database. It does all of the searching, so you don't have to. Queries are going to be one of the biggest things that help to make your database powerful. A query is going to refer to the action that is needed to retrieve data from your database.

In many cases, you are going to be selective when it comes to how much data you would like returned. If you have a lot of data that is present in that database, you probably don't want to look through all of the information. You likely have some kind of criteria that you would like to work with, and you only want to bring up the data that matches.

For example, you may want to take a look through your database and see how many individuals in that database live in one city, or in one geographical area. Or you may want to see the time period of when different individuals registered with your database in a given time period. You can submit a query to help you discover all of this information.

The database that is used in data science is going to be quite large and making sure that you only get the information that you want out of it, rather than having to search through and figure out what answers fit and what don't, can be so important in terms of getting accurate insights. As with many of the other tasks that you can do with programming, you can do a query of your database either through the user interface or programmatically.

The first option is going to be querying programmatically. This approach is like the example that we talked about earlier, where we worked with the SELECT command. You would use that command in your command prompt and then add in the information about what you would like to retrieve out of the database. This is a quick option to work with and is often going to bring up the answers that you want, without having to do a ton of coding or a lot of searching around or changing up the parameters.

As we talked about, SQL is a powerful language that you can work with, and even though the statement that we wrote above earlier was simple and easy to read even, it is going to bring up all of the information that you need out of the database. You can add in any kind of information and further criteria that are needed, and it is possible to take this further and work with more than one table at the same time, as long as it is in the same database. It really is that simple to work with!

Then we can move on to the second option that is available. You may find in some cases that doing the SQL language is not the option that you like, and you would rather work with the user interface to generate your queries. This is usually the option that programmers are going to work with if they notice their query is going to be more complex than what we have talked about before.

Systems for database management are going to make it easy to work with this kind of thing because they offer a design view for the queries that you want to use. This design view is going to enable you to pick and choose out which columns you would like to display, and which criteria are needed to help filter out all of the data that is found inside your database. Working with this design view can be easier and helps you to sort through the multitude of data in your database to find exactly what you would like.

The user interface that you are going to use with some of your queries will depend on the kind of database that you are using. Some are going to be easier for people to use, such as the options that come with Microsoft Access, but others may prefer that you work with coding and want you to work with this option in order to get the results that you want. You may need to consider which one you would like to work with before starting to ensure that you know what options you have and can choose the one that allows programming in the way that you would like.

These databases are going to be important to some of the work that you do with data science. They are going to allow you to put your data in a form that is easier to look over and digest. While it may not be able to make it as easy to read through as some of the data visualizations that we talked about, it helps to get all of the information in one place, helps you to see what is there, and can even make it easier to figure out if something is missing out of the information. You can then modify and change up the information and the data that is there, and then use the information to complete your analysis and your visualizations to use later on.

In many cases, when you are working with data science, you are going to run across times when you need to put your information into a database, and then search through all of that information in order to find what is most helpful to you. Actively looking through the database when there are hundreds of thousands, and maybe even millions, of points in there can take way too long, and you are going to miss out on the key information that you are really looking for in that database.

When we can work with the query as we have done above, either programmatically or with the user interface, this makes this task much easier to handle. You will get to go through and do a search for the relevant information that you need, rather than having to search through all of the listings that are there. This can limit some of the work that you do, keeps the results that you are looking at down to the minimum of what you actually need, and can provide you with a better opportunity to handle your data and get some good insights in the process.

Chapter 8: A Look at Artificial Intelligence

While we are on the topic of data science, we need to take a little detour and talk about one of the topics that have really helped to grow and develop data science in a new way. Without this kind of industry, it would be really hard for data scientists to go through and actually do some of the work that they need to and see success in the process too. The field that we are talking about here is going to be artificial intelligence.

To start with, AI, or artificial intelligence, is going to be an area of computer science that helps us to emphasize the creation of various machines and systems (based on our needs), that are intelligent, and that we can act and react in a manner that is pretty much identical to how humans view the world and react to it as well. There are different activities, powered by machine learning algorithms that we will talk about in a bit, that can help out with this. Some of the activities that smart and intelligence computers can do with the help of artificial intelligence include speech recognition, planning problem solving, and learning.

With this in mind, any time that you are doing some work with artificial intelligence, we are basically in the world of computer science, which is part of what we need to make data science so powerful. With this subset of computer science though, we want to focus on the processes and the models that are used to teach a machine how to act and think all on its own, without any intervention from humans.

There is a lot of power that is behind these kinds of systems, and it is not always as easy as it may seem. But because of all this power, artificial intelligence is now seen as an essential part of our technology industry, and many companies and businesses are willing to learn how to use it, or at least hire others who are experts at using it for all of their data science needs.

Research that has been done on AI is specialized and highly technical. This could be due to the nature of how artificial intelligence is going to work and all of the different parts that come with it. Some of the core problems that come with the AI include programming the computer for a certain trait including the ability to move and manipulate a variety of objects, learning, perception, planning, knowledge, problem-solving, and reasoning.

Knowledge is going to be powerful when it comes to working with artificial intelligence, and this knowledge engineering is going to be part of the core of research in this field. Machines are often able to learn how to act and react as a human does, but only if they have been given enough information about how the world works, and how they should behave.

Remember, with artificial intelligence, the computer isn't just sitting there and gaining knowledge without any help. The computer is going to be limited based on the information and examples that you present to it, and the learning that it is able to do during this time. If the wrong answers and examples are given to the system, or it is not trained in the proper manner, then this can be a big problem. The machine has to have accurate information, and lots of it, in order to behave and react in a way that is similar to what we see with humans.

To ensure that the work we do with artificial intelligence actually provides help, the computer has to be active. It isn't just sitting there in the background, gaining random knowledge and hoping that all of this works out in the end. Rather, you have to come in and tell it what information you want it to learn from. This helps to keep it in order and makes sure that the program or the machine is able to learn exactly what you want it to know, and it will behave the way that you would like.

As we will explore in a few pages, machine learning is going to be another piece of the puzzle when it comes to artificial intelligence. Machine learning is a subset of artificial intelligence that includes a lot of the algorithms and models that you need to teach the machine. These algorithms can see patterns in the data and can help us to sort through complex and large amounts of data in hardly any time at all.

But to keep us on track and to make sure that things are as simple as possible, artificial intelligence is there to help make it easier for programmers and professionals to train machines to act on their own. These machines can learn how to do this by taking their past experiences, and then adjusts based on the new inputs that it receives over time. Most of the examples that come up when we search about artificial intelligence are going to rely on deep learning and natural language processing, but there are some exceptions to this. When we use either of these two technologies, or any of the other parts that come with artificial intelligence, in the work that we do, it simply means that we are training the computer and machine on how to act simply by training it with a lot of data as examples, and the right kind of algorithm.

Artificial intelligence is important because it is able to help businesses and programmers do a lot of different tasks. For example, artificial intelligence is able to step in and automate some of the learning that becomes repetitive and can help us find more discoveries than ever before when searching through our data. This technology can also go through many tasks and get them done in a timely manner, saving up resources, and giving us the insights that we need into a lot of different things at the same time.

In addition, you can use artificial intelligence to make sure that a product that you already sell (or offer to sell) is able to add in more intelligence; in most cases, you will not get this kind of technology with the help of just one application. Rather, the products that you already use are going to see artificial intelligence improving them and making life easier. Many different smart machines, for example, can be combined together with all of the data that is owned by the company to help us improve the technology we are already using, no matter what field of work you are in.

AI is going to be able to adapt through the progressive learning algorithms so that the data gets to do the programming. AI is able to find any of the regularities or the structure in data so that the algorithm is able to gain a new skill. This algorithm is going to turn into either a predictor or a classifier. So, just like we see the algorithm being able to teach itself the right steps to playing chess, it is also able to use this kind of idea in order to recommend which product the customer should purchase next.

And then the models are going to be able to adapt when they are given the new data. Backpropagation is going to be one of the techniques that AI uses in order to make sure that the chosen model is able to adjust, through training and added data if you find that the first answer that is given does not seem right.

AI is then able to analyze deeper data and more of it with the help of neural networks that have a lot of hidden layers. For example, working with a system for detecting fraud was impossible a few years ago, but with the help of good computer power, AI, and some big data, it is something that many banks and financial institutions can concentrate on. Of course, to make sure that this kind of model will work, it needs a lot of data to be trained on. In fact, the more data that you can feed in, the more accurate these models will end up being.

Next on the list: AI is going to be really accurate at what it does with the help of the deep neural networks, something that was pretty much impossible before. For example, any of the interactions that you do with Alexa, and other similar products, are going to be based on the things that we can do with deep learning. The more that we use them, the more accuracy is going to show up in them as well.

When we compare this to some of the other methods that are available for us to use in data science, the ones that are trying to help with sorting and analyzing the data so that we can understand it better, AI is going to be the best method to use, because it is the most efficient at sorting through the information, and seeing what is there.

You will be surprised at how the answers that your system needs will already be found inside the data, we just need to be able to take the right steps to find this information and the insights that may be hidden inside. There are other options to use to make this happen. But artificial intelligence - and a lot of the algorithms that come with artificial intelligence and machine learning - makes us more effective at getting this all done.

Artificial intelligence has a good space in the world of data science. It can definitely help the data scientist to get their work done in a manner that is more efficient and faster at the same time. There are occasions where other methods are going to be the best, but often (when it comes right down to it), when you want to get accurate insights that drive your business forward and helps you to make good and sound business decisions in a timely manner, artificial intelligence is the right option for you.

Chapter 9: What is Machine Learning and How Is It Different from Artificial Intelligence?

One subset of artificial intelligence that we need to take a look at is the idea of machine learning. This is going to be a method of data analysis that can be helpful because it will automate what happens when we build an analytical model. Remember earlier in data science, we talked about needing models and algorithms to help us get through all of that data and then do an analysis? The process of machine learning is where we come up with those models and then use them!

Machine learning is going to be one of the branches that we see with artificial intelligence. This means that it is a type of artificial intelligence, but it is not the same and will not encompass all of the same parts as artificial intelligence does. This branch is going to be based on the idea that a system can learn from the data it is presented with, it can identify patterns, and it is able to make some smart decisions based on the data you present to it, with little human intervention in the process.

Because of a lot of the new technologies out there for computing, machine learning today has changed quite a bit. It was born from the idea of recognizing patterns, and the idea that a computer or another system would be able to learn, without the programming going in and coding for the specific tasks. Those who wanted to do research and experiment with this idea wanted to take artificial intelligence a bit further and see if a computer was able to learn from the data and do things on its own.

There is a type of iterative aspect to this machine learning, and this is important to the process because as the models are exposed to some new data, they will be able to make the right adaptations, all on their own. This is pretty amazing to consider. The machine is basically able to learn from the computations it did earlier in order to produce decisions and results that are reliable and that you can repeat. It is not a brand-new science to work with, but with some of the new ideas and technologies that come with it today, it has definitely gained a lot of momentum in the process.

While many of the algorithms that work with machine learning have been around us for a number of years now, there are some changes that have made it even more fun to learn about today. The ability for this kind of learning to automatically apply mathematical calculations that are complex too big data (which is what we really need it to do when we work in data science), over and over while getting faster in the process, is a more recent development. There are a lot of different ways that this machine learning can already be used, and that we already see it used in our daily lives, and these include:

The self-driving Google car is currently one of the biggest examples of machine learning at work.

Any of the online recommendations or offers that we see on various websites as we shop.

Machine learning is able to work with something known as linguistic rule creation to help companies know what customers and others are saying on Twitter and other social media accounts.

Fraud detection has been in use with financial institutions for some time now, and when it is powered by machine learning, we are going to see some great results.

All of the new interest that has come with machine learning is due to some of the same factors that have made data mining - and other parts of data science - so important in our modern world. Things like the growing amount and the different types of data that companies can get their hands on have helped to raise some of the interest. Add in that the processing power for doing the computations is cheaper and more powerful than ever before. Also, companies are finding new and innovative ways to store the data; it is no wonder that machine learning and artificial intelligence are two parts of data science that are really growing.

With this in mind, there are a few things that you need to have in place in order to create a system of machine learning that is actually good. You need to make sure that the system has some capabilities to help with data preparation. You need a combination of algorithms that are more advanced, as well as some of the more basic ones as well. You need to have some processes that are iterative and some processes that help with automation. You need scalability in the program so it can handle the larger forms of data that come into a company. You need to have something known as ensemble modeling.

Before we move on from here, there are a few different parts that come with machine learning that we need to focus on for a few minutes. To start, when we work with machine learning, the target is going to be called a label. But in statistics, the target goes by another name of a dependent variable. That variable in statistics is going to be a feature when we go back to machine learning and use statistics in there.

As you can imagine, there are already a lot of companies who are using machine learning. Pretty much anyone who is adding in some data science to their mix and trying to do data analysis of all that information will use machine learning. Machine learning provides them with the models they need during this process, models that can help them actually sort through the information and find the results they need.

This means that the financial world, the government, health care, retail, oil and gas, and transportation are all going to benefit when we can create machine learning algorithms that work well with them.

Any industry that is trying to beat out the competition, provide better customer service, and make better decisions based on the data they have collected will be able to use machine learning to their advantage.

For example, government agencies can use this kind of process and the algorithms that come with machine learning in order to help them provide more utilities and public safety to those around them. Government agencies are going to have many different sources of data that they need to first mine through in order to find all of the insights that are there. As an example, they could take some time to monitor and analyze the data in the sensors for traffic signals, and then use these to help them keep the signals going at the right times, getting people to the right location in the most efficient manner as possible.

Another area that we haven't discussed much in data science but can use the algorithms of machine learning will be oil and gas. This is especially important when we are looking at finding new sources of energy. The algorithms of machine learning will be able to analyze minerals found in the ground; they can predict how likely it is that the sensor in the refinery will fail. They can streamline the oil distribution to make it more cost-effective and efficient, and more. This is definitely an industry that is going to benefit well when it comes to using machine learning.

While there are a lot of different industries that are going to benefit when it comes to using machine learning, we can see how many of them work in the field of data science; they work pretty much the same with machine learning. We will on to some of the methods of machine learning that are common and popular in helping get things done.

There are many options that programmers can go with when it comes to using machine learning. Each of the algorithms is set up to take on different types of tasks, which makes them helpful for all of the different things you would like to do in data science. Even so, it is possible to separate out the algorithms into four general categories, based on the way they teach the system or computer how to behave.

The four methods of machine learning that we are going to use to classify our algorithms will include supervised machine learning, semi-supervised machine learning, unsupervised machine learning, and reinforcement learning. All of these are going to work in a slightly different manner, so let's take some time to explore them and see how they can work for any of our machine learning needs.

The first option on the list is going to be supervised learning. These are the algorithms that are going to be trained using examples that have been labeled. We are basically showing the system a lot of different examples of how it should work, and what answers are going to be true and which ones are going to be false. Then when we are done showing all of these examples, we can then do a test to see who often the computer system is able to make these predictions, based on what they were shown to start with.

In supervised machine learning, the input is going to be provided based on a known desired output. You may have a machine or a piece of equipment, for example, that has data points labeled either R for runs or F for failed. The learned algorithm is going to be able to receive in a set of inputs, and along with these inputs, they will get the right outputs that go along with them. The algorithm can then use this information to learn by comparing the actual output with the correct output to find the errors that are there. The model will then be modified according to the results the system has found.

Through a variety of different methods, like predictions, classifications, regressions, and gradient boosting, this kind of learning algorithm is going to use patterns to help it come up with a good prediction of the values of a label on any data that comes in later that does not have a label. Often, we will work with this kind of learning with an application where historical data can predict how likely it is that an event in the future will happen. A good example of this would be when a financial institution uses machine learning in order to tell whether a transaction on a credit card is legitimate or if there is some fraudulent activity going on with the card.

Then we can move on to what is known as semi-supervised learning. This one is going to be pretty similar to the supervised machine learning, and often they will just be grouped together rather than having them as two different categories. Semi-supervised machine learning is going to work with a lot of the same applications that we will find with supervised learning as well. So, why would we want to take some time to talk about another application that is pretty similar to what we have already discussed?

With semi-supervised machine learning, we will find that the algorithm will use a combination of unlabeled and labeled data to help with training. There is usually just a tiny amount of data that is labeled to help things along, with the majority of the data you feed in being unlabeled. The reason that we focus on just a bit of the labeled data is that it is expensive, and it takes more time to acquire. But when we work primarily with the unlabeled data, we can still get the algorithm to work, for a lot less money and it takes a lot less effort in the process to get it all done.

This type of learning is going to use a lot of the same methods of learning to get things done as supervised learning, including using the methods of regression, classification, and prediction. This is also useful when we see the cost of labeling the data points is too high for us to use in the labeled training process. A good example of how this has been used so far is with programs that can use a webcam to recognize the face of the other person.

In addition to the two types of supervised learning, we need to take a moment to discuss a bit more about unsupervised machine learning. This is going to provide more power to the various programs that we want to create but will work in a manner that is a little bit different than all of the others. This kind of learning is different from the other two in that it is able to use data that does not have a label on it in order to learn and complete its tasks.

The goal here is for the algorithm to figure out what kind of information is being shown. We want to be able to explore the data and find if there is some structure inside of it. One way we can see how unsupervised machine learning is able to work is with transactional data. What we mean here is that these algorithms can help a company identify segments of customers who have attributes that are similar, and who the company can treat in a similar manner when they complete a marketing campaign.

Or, you can use these algorithms to help find out which attributes are important for separating out your customers into various segments from one another. These are just a few of the examples, and you will find that unsupervised machine learning can often be used when you want to go through large amounts of data with data science.

You get some options when it comes to working with the unsupervised machine learning algorithms. Some of the methods that are the most popular are going to include clustering, nearest-neighbor mapping, maps that self-organize, and more. These are the types of algorithms that come into play when you would like to figure out more about the outliers in your set of data, list out items that are recommended to your customers based on their past history, and segment topics of the text.

And the fourth type of machine learning that we can focus on is reinforcement learning. To those who have not had much time to explore machine learning and all that it entails, you will find that reinforcement sometimes acts in a manner that is similar to what we discussed in unsupervised machine learning. While the outward appearance is maybe going to look similar, the stuff that goes on behind the scenes and the things that put this kind of algorithm into motion will be different than what you see with the unsupervised machine learning algorithms we talked about before.

This kind of algorithm is something that we often see in gaming, robotics, and navigation. With reinforcement learning, the algorithm is going to be able to discover, using the process of trial and error, which actions out of a set of choices will provide you with the best rewards to the minimum amount of risks in the process.

When we work with reinforcement machine learning, we will find that there are going to be three components that have to show up to make it work. We will start out with the first component of the agent, who is the decision-maker or the learning in this process.

Then we have the environment, which will include everything that our agent from before is able to interact with. Finally, we end with actions, which will be what our agent is able to do.

The whole objective of doing this work is for the agent to go through and pick out the right actions, ensuring that they can maximize the expected reward over a given amount of time. The agent is going to be able to achieve this kind of goal much faster when they follow a good policy. What this means for us is that the agent is going to be able to reach their goal much faster when they can follow a good policy, and we can use this kind of learning to help make that happen.

The differences between deep learning, machine learning, and data mining

With all of this in mind, we are going to take a look at how this process is different compared to some of the other topics we have discussed in this guidebook. This will help us to see some more of the results that we would like and makes it easier to really complete some of the parts of data science in the manner that we should.

These three topics have the same goal: extract relationships, patterns, and insights useful in making company decisions. All three of them are going to be different in that they will use different abilities and different approaches to help them reach their goals.

First, let's go back to data mining from before. We can consider this data mining as a kind of superset of many different methods that are used to extract some good insights out of our data. It could often involve some of the algorithms, as well as some of the traditional statistical methods, that are used in machine learning. Data mining is going to work to apply methods from many areas the number and type depending on what the end goal is, to help make our set of data and identify the patterns that we did not know before.

There are a lot of methods that come into play when doing the process of data mining. Of course, machine learning is part of this, but if the data requires some other method to help out, then this is available to data mining as well. Some of the methods and areas that data mining is able to work from will include time series analysis, text analytics, machine learning, and statistical algorithms. Data mining can also go a bit further in that it includes the study and the practice of data manipulation and data storage.

Then we move on to machine learning from here. The main difference that we are going to see with machine learning is that, just like what we see with models of statistics, the goal is to understand some of the structure that is seen with the data. We want to fit theoretical distributions to the data that are already well understood. So, with the idea of statistical models, there is going to be a theory behind the model that has been proven by mathematical facts so far, but this requires that the data has to be able to meet up with some assumptions that are pretty strong as well.

The development of machine learning is based on the ability we have to use computers to probe the data for structure, even if we start out having no theory of what our structure needs to look like. The test that we can run for a model of machine learning is a validation error on new data, rather than a theoretical test that is going to prove a null hypothesis. Because this kind of learning is able to be more iterative than others when it learns from the data at hand, the learning can be something that we automate, rather than having to focus on it all of the time. Passes are run through the data until we can find a good robust pattern to work with.

And finally, we need to take a look at deep learning. Deep learning is a bit different than what we see with the other two processes, but it is still important. This deep learning is going to combine together some of the advances that we see with computing power and special types of neural networks and have both learn complicated patterns in large amounts of data.

The techniques that you are going to see with deep learning are going to be considered state of the art for identifying objects in images, and even words in sounds. Researchers at this time are looking to find new and exciting ways to apply these successes in pattern recognition to some tasks that may be more complex.

Some of the tasks that we can use deep learning with, especially when it comes to pattern recognition, can include things like medical diagnoses, automatic language translation, and other problems of social and business nature that are important. The possibilities are endless when it comes to this one, which is part of why this industry is such a great one to spend our time learning about and perfecting into the future.

While all three of these options, from data mining to machine learning to deep learning are different, they can all work on the same goal to help us see the success that we would like. Learning how to combine them together, and when to pull each one out at the right time can be the difference between failure and success with our data science endeavor.

Basically, machine learning is going to be important here because it helps us to really take a closer look at the data we have, using algorithms that can quickly and efficiently find the patterns and hidden information that we want within the set of data. The way that this does its job will often depend on the kind of learning that you do, what information you would like to get out of it, and whether the data is labeled for this kind of process or not.

While data science is something that handles all aspects of collecting the data, looking it over, and then exploring what we can do with that information, machine learning is just going to focus on what we need to do to see what is inside our set of data. With a list of algorithms to help you out, you will find that it is easier to really get into that data and see the best predictions that you need to make smart decisions, ones that help your business to grow and your bottom line to rise.

Chapter 10: What is the Future of Artificial Intelligence and Machine Learning?

In this guidebook, we have spent some time looking at the different parts that come with data science. There are definitely a lot of them that come together and help us to work on so many amazing projects over time. We looked at what data mining and data analysis are all about. We examined data querying to see how this could fit into the puzzle. We considered the topics of artificial intelligence and machine learning as well.

With this in mind, it is time to see some of the things that could come in the future when we look towards artificial intelligence and data science as a whole. There are already many industries who are using this kind of technology to help propel themselves into the future, so it makes sense that this technology would continue to grow, and we will see even more amazing things in the process.

In our current world, we can see a lot of examples of artificial intelligence already. We see smart homes where we can control our televisions, our light systems, our thermostats and more all with the help of our voice we use our smartphones and other devices to help give us directions and tell us other information that we want to know. We use search engines to look at the recommendations that companies give us and see all of the advertisements that are posted on a regular basis. Artificial intelligence, whether we realize it or not, is already a big part of our lives and the role that it takes is likely to get bigger as time goes on.

The future of artificial intelligence is exciting, and there is so much potential based on how people continue to look at this technology, and what the data scientists and other engineers work to produce. Many businesses are already looking favorably on this kind of technology, which means it is likely this will continue to grow quite a bit in the future.

Right now, the biggest concern that is out there about artificial intelligence, that is legitimate, is that there won't be enough professionals out there to handle the new technology. Companies are excited to jump on board with some of the technology and see what it has to offer. But they worry that they would not be able to find enough professionals to help run and manage that technology, and enough professionals to read through all of the data that comes with that new technology.

We also have to look at the fact that there will be a few jobs replaced with this kind of technology as time goes on as well. These are not going to be enough that we are going to all be homeless or worried about how to split up the money generated by machines. But it can be helpful when it comes to areas where there is an employee shortage going around. This can affect a lot of different industries, but one place where it seems like it is going to have a big impact in terms of jobs in the healthcare industry.

As our population ages, there are worries that there will not be enough personnel to help handle all of the tasks that need to be done. It may be difficult finding enough people to help with administrative duties, enough nurses to handle all of the shifts and take care of people in their homes. Likewise, doctors are likely to feel overwhelmed and overworked in the process as they try to keep up with all of the patients they need to see. This is a lot of strain on an industry that is important, and one that all of us want to see working properly when we need it most.

This is likely a field where artificial intelligence is really going to take off. We can use the ideas behind artificial intelligence to help us deal with some of the shortages that may fall in this industry, picking up some of the empty spaces with the jobs, helping medical professionals do their jobs more efficiently even with fewer of them, so this industry can continue to thrive.

The healthcare field is not the only place that will be able to benefit from the use of artificial intelligence. Many other industries are going to use this to help them stay on top of things, to help them gain a competitive advantage, and to make it easier for them to serve their customers. We can see this in the financial industry and how they use this kind of technology to help approve loans, finding financial crime and fraud, and so much more.

Pretty much any organization, no matter what industry they are in, can benefit when they see more productivity in their work, and this is something that can be done with the automation of artificial intelligence. When the automation is done in the proper way, it is going to help them generate more revenue in the process, providing them with additional money to use on new products and for supporting jobs to do even better.

There are a few different ways that we can take some of the features and capabilities that we see with artificial intelligence and use it in our business. Due to some of the jobs that we are going to see impacted through this technology, it is important for us also to stop and address the pitfalls that are potentially there as well. There are a few things that could be considered pitfalls, and as such, we really need to take a look at them as well. Some of these potential pitfalls are going to include:

Businesses have to be able to overcome some of the bias and trust issues that are often going to come with AI by achieving an effective and successful implementation, making it possible for all of the people using the system to benefit in the process.

The governments who use this need to ensure that any gains they get from Ai can be shared widely, or as much as possible, across the whole of society to prevent social inequality between those affected and those who unaffected by these developments. For example, this could be through increased investment in the training to make it happen.

With some of the additional cost savings that happen with implementing the AI systems, employers need to also focus on increasing the number of skills that their current, and future employees need to have.

To properly leverage a lot of the power of AI, we need to be able to address some of the issues that happen at an educational level, as well as the business. Education systems need to be able to use this in order to focus on being able to train students in the roles directly associated with working on AI and can include people like data analysts and programmers. This means that there needs to be some more emphasis to be put on STEM subjects so that this can be handled in the process as well.

Also, we need to take some time to center around building emotional, social, and creative skills that need to be encouraged. Artificial intelligence may be more productive than the human workers in terms of some repetitive tasks. That said, humans can outperform machines in jobs requiring a lot of imagination (or building relationships), which is going to help improve jobs in this sector.

At the same time, you will find that a future involving artificial intelligence is likely to make some big changes in our world, both inside and outside. It is likely that some of these major changes are happening behind the scenes, without us even realizing what is going on. Before we know it, more products and services will be released, or at least created, with the help of this artificial intelligence to keep them going.

Now that we have a bit of background on artificial intelligence and some of the possibilities involved when this technology takes off, let's look at some of the potential options for artificial intelligence that are already making their way onto the market. Some of the most promising, and the most popular, of these future applications of artificial intelligence will include sectors mentioned below.

Automated Transportation

We already see this a bit with the help of cars that are self-driving, though the vehicles will still need to have a driver present to make sure that things are safe. Despite this new development, the idea of automated transportation is still new, and it may take a bit before it gets safe enough to use and will take even longer before it is accepted by the public.

Google began testing a self-driving car in 2012, and since this time, the U.S. Department of Transportation has seen so much that is going on has released definitions of the types and levels of automation, and the car from Google is one of the first levels and then it goes all the way down to full automation. There are also some other methods here that we can use, ones that are going to be closer to some of the full automation, such as trains and buses. It is likely that this is going to grow more in the future and be part of the way that we travel.

Seeing the Robots as Friends

In reality, who wouldn't want to have a friend that is a robot? Okay, most people would probably not want this, and they may wish to stay away from this as much as possible. Still, this is something we are likely to see as our future as AI becomes more prevalent in our daily lives. Right now, the great majority of robots are emotionless; it's hard to picture an emotionless robot that you can relate to and be friendly with.

This is something that is going to change in the future, though. There is a company in Japan that has been able to make significant progress in terms of a robot companion we might enjoy having around. This companion would be able to understand and even feel some emotions. In fact, "Pepper" is a companion robot that went on sale in 2015 and had 1,000 units sell out in just a minute! For this robot, we saw that it had been programmed in order to read the emotions of humans and even to develop some of its own emotions.

Pepper was created to make sure that its human friends would stay happy.

While this still has a long way to go, and it is likely that this kind of machine is not going to be able to replace human interaction or fully understand emotions, it is pretty neat what technology can do right now. We may be able to take a computer program and use AI and machine learning in order to teach it how to relate to humans, have some emotions, and really be a companion that we can rely on.

Cyborg Technology

One of the main limitations of being human is our own brains and our own bodies. According to one researcher, Shimon Whiteson, in the future, we are going to be able to augment ourselves with the help of computers – computers that don't replace us, but instead will *enhance* some of our own natural abilities. Though many of these enhancements would just be done for convenience in most cases, other times they could come on board to serve a purpose that is more practical.

It has been noted that AI is going to become more useful for several people who have amputated limbs and who would like to be able to walk around and move with some of the same capabilities that they did in the past. With the help of AI, this cyborg technology is going to be able to allow the brain to communicate with the limb in order to allow the patient the control that they need over that limb. This technology could work in several different ways, but it is going to reduce some of the limitations that an amputee is going to deal with on a daily basis.

This is just the beginning of what we are likely to see when it comes to artificial intelligence in the future. Many companies and individuals are likely to take this kind of information and technology and use it in order to really grow and beat out the competition. The types of products that we are likely to get out of the process are going to be so different from what we can imagine today. This can be an exciting thing to think about!

Conclusion

Thank you for making it through to the end of *Data Science*, let's hope it was informative and able to provide you with all of the tools you need to achieve your goals whatever they may be.

The next step is to start taking a look at some of the different ways that you can use data science in your own life. There are a lot of different aspects that come with this process, and often it is so important that there are not enough professionals out there to help with all of the demand. Many times, it is hard to understand what this process is even all about, much less why it is so important, and the goal of this guidebook was to help us really gain a good understanding of what this data science is all about.

Many companies are spending here time collecting data and gathering it from a variety of sources, whether it is online, social media, in person, about the industry, or through a survey. While it is great that these companies are being proactive and trying to learn as much about their customers, their competition, and their business as possible, all of this data is worthless if we can't take a look at the data and learn what is hidden inside. This is exactly what data science is all about.

With all of that data, it is easy for information to get hidden deep inside and being able to sort through all of that information and find the hidden trends and the useful information to help make sound business decisions is a big challenge. A data scientist is able to use various algorithms and methods from machine learning and artificial intelligence in order to find out this information and present it in a manner that is easy to understand.

In this guidebook, we looked at many of the different aspects that came with artificial intelligence and discussed how it could be used in order to help companies provide better customer service, design the right products that will be able to sell, and so much more. It is likely that this data can take on more of a role in business decisions and other aspects of the business as time goes on.

Before any of this can happen though, we need to have data science come out to help and show us just what information is hiding in all of that data. A good data scientist will be able to get through all of the information and learn what is found inside data that might be hiding it all.

When you are ready to learn more about data science and what it can do for many companies, no matter what industry they are in, make sure to check out this guidebook to help you get started.

Finally, if you found this book useful in any way, a review on Amazon is always appreciated!

Here are other books by Richard Hurley

BIG DATA

A Guide to Big Data Trends, Artificial Intelligence,
Machine Learning, Predictive Analytics,
Internet of Things, Data Science, Data Analytics,
Business Intelligence, and Data Mining

RICHARD HURLEY